D0962534

RPM

RACECARS

The Ins and Outs of *Stock Cars, Dragsters,*
and *Open-Wheelers*

By Sean McCollum

Consultant:
Tony Thacker
Executive Director
Wally Parks NHRA Motorsports Museum
Pomona, California

Capstone
press®
Mankato, Minnesota

Velocity is published by Capstone Press,
151 Good Counsel Drive, P.O. Box 669, Mankato, Minnesota 56002.
www.capstonepress.com

Books published by Capstone Press are manufactured with paper
containing at least 10 percent post-consumer waste.

Library of Congress Cataloging-in-Publication Data
McCollum, Sean.
    Racecars: the ins and outs of stock cars, dragsters, and open wheelers /
by Sean McCollum.
    p. cm. — (Velocity. RPM)
    Includes bibliographical references and index.
    Summary: "Includes details about the history and current status of racecars, including
stock cars, dragsters, and open-wheelers" — Provided by publisher.
    ISBN 978-1-4296-3429-8 (library binding)
    1. Automobiles, Racing — Juvenile literature. I. Title. II. Series.
TL236.M3728 2010
629.228 — dc22   2009002182

Editorial Credits
Mandy Robbins, editor; Ashlee Suker, designer; Jo Miller, media researcher

Photo Credits
Alamy/pbpgalleries, 5 (inset)
AP Images, 4–5, 6–7
Getty Images for NASCAR/Jeff Zelevansky, 45 (Richard Petty)
Getty Images Inc./Alvis Upitis, 8; Jamie Squire, 20–21; Racing One, 9, 12–13, 14–15 (both),
    41; Reporter Images, 38–39; Rusty Jarrett, 28
Newscom, 17 (HANS device), 22, 26, 27, 34 (junior drag racer), 36–37, 42–43; ABACAUSA/
    Cal Sport Media, 18–19; CSM/Christopher Szagola, 31; Icon SMI/David Allio, 32, 35, 44;
    Jared C. Tilton/ASP Inc, 11; Splash News/A&E/Taylor Jones, 29
Shutterstock/Christopher Halloran, 16–17; craig hill, 24–25 (Indy car); Dario Sabljak,
    10 (boxing gloves); Derek Yegan, 30–31 (top), 33; Graham Bloomfield, 23;
    john j. klaiber jr., 45 (sprint car); kozvic49, 20 (checkered flag); kRie, 24–25 (F1 car);
    Orange Line Media, 10 (main image); Rafa Irusta, cover; STU, 40

Design Elements
iStockphoto/kativ
Shutterstock/ArchMan; Betacam-SP; Gordan; High Leg Studio; Lori Carpenter; Nicemonkey

TABLE OF CONTENTS

RACECARS 101

It was called the Blitzen Benz. *Blitzen* is German for "lightning." Benz was the German company that built the car. Like other early racecars, the Blitzen Benz looked like a sub sandwich on spoked wheels.

It may not have looked like today's cars, but in 1910, it was the fastest car around. Its huge engine produced 200 horsepower. The rest of the car was built around its engine. Like a bicycle, the car used a chain drive to transfer power from the engine to its rear wheels.

Barney Oldfield

This car helped turn American Barney Oldfield into one of the first stars of racing. He had already set speed records in other cars. He later drove in the first Indianapolis 500 in 1911.

Oldfield liked to put on a show. He would drive into a town and challenge local drivers to race. Crowds gathered at the local horse racing track for the contest. There, Oldfield kicked up the dirt and left the other drivers in the dust.

In 1910, Oldfield took the Blitzen Benz to the sand flats of Daytona Beach, Florida. There, he set a speed record of 131 miles (211 kilometers) per hour. A year later, the Blitzen Benz reached 141 miles (227 kilometers) per hour. That record stood for nine years. But it was just a hint of the roaring cars to come.

A few Blitzen Benz models are still running today.

A TIME LINE OF RACECARS

1885 German inventor Karl Benz builds the first commercial car.

1895 First car race is held in France.

1906 First Grand Prix is held in France.

1911 First Indianapolis 500 is held (pictured).

1929 First Monaco Grand Prix is held.

1948 NASCAR is formed to organize stock car racing.

1950 First drag strip is opened in California.

1959 First Daytona 500 is held; Lee Petty wins in a photo finish.

1960 Shift from front-engine to rear-engine Grand Prix cars

1969 Airfoils first appear on Formula One cars.

Modern racecars have come a long way since the Blitzen Benz. They are sleeker, to help slice through the air. They are made with lighter, stronger materials. Their engines produce a lot more power, and they are much safer for drivers.

Today's racecars have also changed depending on what event they compete in. Top fuel dragsters look like darts on wheels. The shape helps them split the air as they go from 0 to 300 miles (483 kilometers) per hour in less than five seconds. Indy and Formula One cars have wings that help hold them to the track.

1977 Janet Guthrie becomes the first woman to drive in the Daytona 500 and the Indianapolis 500. Drag racer Shirley Muldowney becomes the first woman to win the Winston World Points Championship.

1997 First supersonic land speed record is set at 766 miles (1,233 kilometers) per hour.

2005 First international NASCAR race is held in Mexico.

2009 The Dakar Rally is held in South America for the first time.

FAMILY HISTORY

Racing has a rich family history. Sons, daughters, and grandchildren of a racer often end up behind the wheel. The Unsers and Andrettis are admired by Indy car fans for generations of top-notch racing.

Mario Andretti (left) and Bobby Unser (right) raced against each other in the 1960s.

The Pettys and Earnhardts are famous in stock car racing. In the 1950s and 1960s, Lee Petty and Ralph Earnhardt lit up the stock car racing circuit. Years later, their sons Richard Petty and Dale Earnhardt Sr. tied for the greatest number of NASCAR points championships ever won.

THE ALLISONS

In the 1950s, brothers Bobby and Donnie Allison began a racing dynasty. Donnie succeeded in racing in NASCAR and Indy car races. Bobby became one of the greatest stars of NASCAR. Bobby's sons Clifford and Davey and his grandson Robbie became racecar drivers as well.

THE FAMILY FORCE

On the drag strip, John Force is a funny car legend. He picked up his love of racing from his uncle Gene Beaver. After 32 years behind the wheel, Force has won 14 funny car championships. Today, Force's daughters, Ashley, Courtney, and Brittany are making names for themselves in drag racing as well.

The Intimidator and Junior

In the 1980s and 1990s, Dale Earnhardt Sr. was known as "the Intimidator." His aggressive driving style helped him win seven NASCAR championships.

Sadly, Earnhardt died in a crash at the 2001 Daytona 500. His death broke the hearts of NASCAR fans.

Earnhardt's son Dale Jr., or "Junior," is now one of NASCAR's brightest stars. When he won the Daytona 500 in 2004, Junior said, "My dad was in the passenger seat right with me today, and I am sure he had a blast."

THE ATHLETE BEHIND THE WHEEL

Stomp on the accelerator and turn the wheel. Some people think that is all it takes to be a racecar driver. But a pro driver's body must be a fine-tuned machine, just like his or her car.

Pro drivers train year-round to increase their performance. They work out to be in tip-top shape. Many drivers lift weights and run.

NASCAR driver Jeff Burton exercises by kickboxing.

Drivers have to stay strong and alert for hours of intense driving. Their hearts beat as fast as the hearts of long-distance runners during a race. They also endure a strong force of gravity pressing on them throughout each race. A driver must have strong stomach and back muscles to withstand that pressure.

"You can be skillful at racing, but if you don't have the strength, you are likely to finish in a poor position with an increased chance of injury from crashing."
— Mark Martin, NASCAR driver

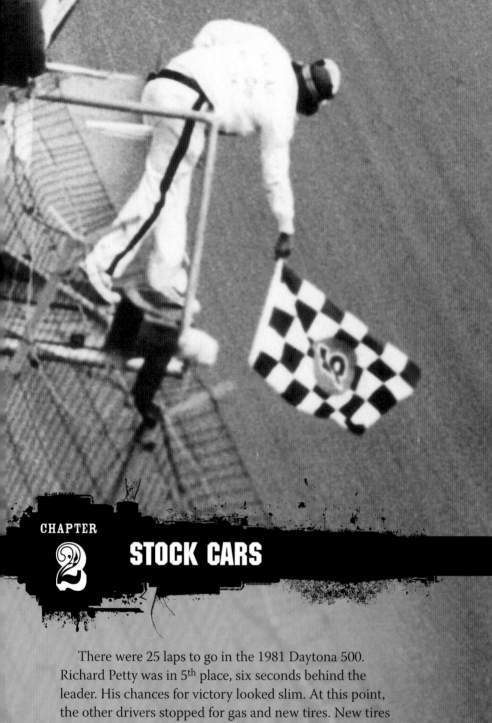

2 STOCK CARS

There were 25 laps to go in the 1981 Daytona 500. Richard Petty was in 5th place, six seconds behind the leader. His chances for victory looked slim. At this point, the other drivers stopped for gas and new tires. New tires would add speed for the last part of the race. Their pit stops took about 17 seconds.

Petty's crew chief, Dale Inman, made a bold decision. In Petty's last pit stop he refueled but kept his old tires. His pit stop only took seven seconds.

When the cars hit the track again, Petty had the lead. His old tires held out, and Petty beat the others by four seconds. "My car was probably the seventh-fastest here, but it was first across the [finish] line," Petty said. "We just out-thunk 'em."

Racing takes more than a fast car and a gutsy driver. It requires strategy and teamwork. Richard Petty's smart racing, combined with a talented pit crew, helped him win a record 200 NASCAR races. That is why he is known as "The King" of stock car racing.

STOCK CARS THEN AND NOW

In the early days of stock car racing, drivers raced regular cars. They were not built specifically for racing. In fact, drivers often drove themselves to races in their stock cars.

The first-ever NASCAR race was held at Daytona Beach in 1948.

In 1948, the National Association for Stock Car Auto Racing (NASCAR) was formed. This organization set rules for stock car races. It promoted safety improvements to protect drivers and fans.

Today, stock car racing is one of the most popular sports in the United States. Millions of fans attend races each year. Even more fans watch major races on TV. Top drivers earn millions of dollars each year.

Professional drivers like Jeff Gordon, Dale Earnhardt Jr., and Tony Stewart battle for points toward NASCAR's Sprint Cup Championship. Races are held on super speedways around the United States. Speeds can reach more than 200 miles (322 kilometers) per hour.

TODAY'S STOCK CARS

Today's stock cars may look somewhat like regular cars, but that is where the similarities end. Under the shell is a pure racing machine.

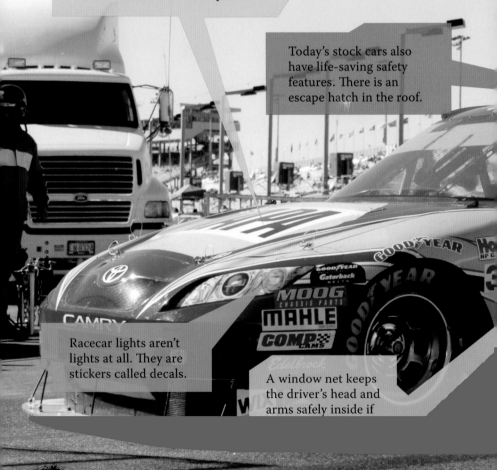

Engineers and mechanics tune the engine to get every ounce of power out of it. Engines can crank out more than 800 horsepower.

Today's stock cars also have life-saving safety features. There is an escape hatch in the roof.

Racecar lights aren't lights at all. They are stickers called decals.

A window net keeps the driver's head and arms safely inside if

Drivers wear safety gear. Their heads are protected by a Head and Neck Support (HANS) device. The HANS device keeps a driver's neck stable in a crash. Drivers also wear fireproof suits and gloves.

Roof flaps and strips keep cars from flying into the air in bad pile-ups.

A roll cage helps protect the driver from getting crushed during a crash.

THE PIT STOP

The pit crew is as important to a good race as the car or driver. Top crews can fill a car with gas and change all four tires in less than 15 seconds. NASCAR allows seven team members to jump over the wall to service a car.

gas man — *fills the car's fuel cell with 48 gallons (182 liters) of racing fuel*

catch can man — *catches the overflow during refueling and signals when refueling is done*

jackman — *uses a jack to raise the car's front and back for tire changes*

support crew — *passes over tires, fuel, and needed equipment from behind the wall*

two tire carriers — *bring new tires to the tire changers*

two tire changers — *one changes the front tires; the other changes the back tires.*

RACING FLAGS

During a NASCAR race, officials use these flags to communicate with drivers.

Flag	Meaning
Green	start or restart of the race
Yellow	drive with caution
Yellow and red stripes	debris or oil on course
Red	stop racing
White	final lap
Black	penalty
Checkered	end of race

DRAFTING

In racing, drivers use certain strategies to get an edge. One of the most common strategies is drafting.

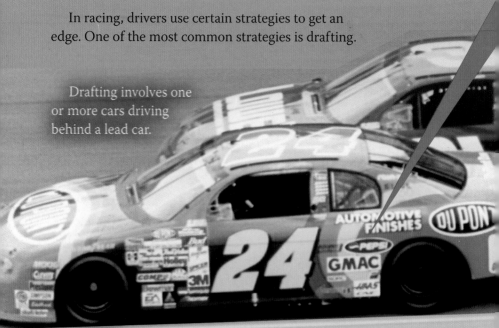

Drafting involves one or more cars driving behind a lead car.

The front car has to push through the most air resistance. This creates calmer air behind it.

RACING SPONSORS

Ever wonder why racecars are plastered with all kinds of decals? Those companies sponsor the racing teams. Sponsors pay a lot of money to advertise on racecars. This money helps the racing teams pay for creating a great car.

Drafting can result in an exciting "slingshot pass." A slingshot pass happens when the airflow shifts as drafting cars round a curve. The trailing car then passes the lead car as they come out of a curve.

The following car pushes air against the rear end of the lead car. This gives the lead car a shove. Two drafting cars can go faster together than one car alone. This technique also saves fuel.

OPEN-WHEEL RACECARS

In 1967, John Surtees won the Italian Grand Prix. Like all the other open-wheel racecars of the time, his car looked like a sub sandwich with big black wheels sticking out of it.

John Surtees drove a Honda RA300 in the 1967 Italian Grand Prix.

Just a year later, Formula One (F1) cars looked very different. Two wings spread from the nose. A larger wing slanted down above the engine in the back.

In racing, big changes often come very fast. Why? When a new car design wins races, other racing teams are quick to copy it. In the late 1960s, open-wheel cars with wings started winning.

What's the deal with those wings? They are like upside down aircraft wings. They push the car down. Wings keep the car glued to the road and steady at high speeds.

2008 F1 Ferrari

F1 racecars are called "open-wheel" because their tires are uncovered. F1 and Indy cars are the most popular cars of this type.

Engine: 2.4-liter V-8
Horsepower: about 750

Top Speed	about 230 miles per hour (370 kilometers)
Weight	1,575 pounds (714 kilograms) for oval tracks 1,640 pounds (744 kilograms) for road courses
Height	38 inches (97 centimeters) maximum

Engine: 3.5-liter V-8
Horsepower: about 650

INDY SERIES CAR

Top Speed	about 225 miles (362 kilometers) per hour
Weight	at least 1,323 pounds (600 kilograms)
Height	37 inches (94 centimeters) maximum

Gearbox: 4 to 7 semi-automatic
forward gears

Fuel: unleaded racing gasoline

Tires: non-grooved racing slicks

Wheelbase: about 122 inches
(310 centimeters)

Gearbox: 6-speed paddle shift

Fuel: fuel-grade ethanol

Tires: grooved racing slicks

Wheelbase: about 120 inches (305 centimeters)

A TRICKY TRADE-OFF

Racing teams work constantly to balance speed and control. Their cars need body designs that cut through the air. This type of design increases speed and uses less fuel. Less fuel use equals fewer pit stops, which means a better chance of winning.

Top quality tires and airfoils help the car grip the track and make the car easier to control. But they also slow down the car and increase fuel use.

Racing teams test their designs on scale models of the cars. The teams put the models in wind tunnels that blast air and smoke. This test lets designers see how well the cars cut through the air.

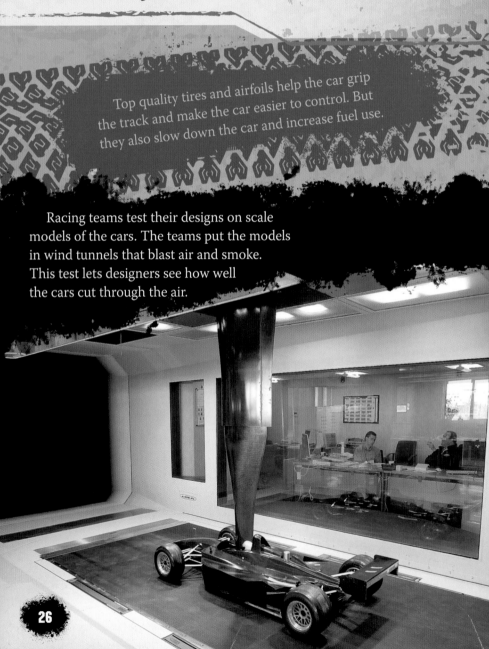

AT THE CONTROLS

The cockpits of today's racecars put drivers in more control than ever before. Dials and buttons on the control panel affect different systems of the car. In a split second, a driver can press a button to increase the car's performance.

Warning lights go on if something is wrong with the car.

With the flick of a switch, drivers can adjust their brakes for different conditions.

Drivers can change the air and fuel mixture to save fuel or increase power.

CHAPTER 4

AT THE DRAG STRIP

In 2008, Ashley Force qualified for the funny car finals at a race in Atlanta, Georgia. Her opponent? Her dad — drag racing legend John Force.

Father and daughter rolled to the starting line side by side. The race lights ticked off three yellows, then flashed green.

Ashley Force drives a Ford Mustang funny car.

The two Forces floored it. In less than five seconds, Ashley was traveling 300 miles (483 kilometers) per hour. She won the race and became the first woman to win a funny car national final.

The Force racing team is one of the most exciting teams in drag racing today. But the sport has enjoyed a long, high-speed history.

Courtney Force

Laurie Force

John Force

Brittany Force

Ashley Force

Drag racing began in California in the 1930s. Young drivers raced souped-up hot rods on country roads and dry lakebeds.

The National Hot Rod Association (NHRA) formed in 1951. Since then, the NHRA has developed competition and safety rules for dragsters. It has worked hard to stop dangerous and illegal street racing.

Strong, light chromoly tubes form the inner "skeleton" of a top fuel dragster.

Top fuelers use a special mix of high-powered fuel called nitromethane.

DRAG RACERS

More than 200 types of vehicles drag race. The three most popular drag racing vehicles are top fuel dragsters, pro stock cars, and funny cars. Today, there are more than 300 drag strips around the world. A drag strip is usually ⅛ mile (.2 kilometer) or ¼ mile (.4 kilometer) long.

TOP FUEL DRAGSTERS

Airfoils help top fuelers grip the track.

Top fuelers reach speeds of more than 330 miles (531 kilometers) per hour.

Top fuelers release parachutes to help them slow down quickly after a wild ride.

The back wheels are large racing slicks. Slicks have no treads. The smooth surface gives them more traction.

The two small front wheels are for steering.

The outer body of a top fueler is built from lightweight aluminum and carbon fiber.

PRO STOCK CARS

Pro stock cars are built differently than stock cars that race in NASCAR events. The most noticeable difference is the tube-like hood scoop that sits in front of the windshield.

Pro stock engines cost about $80,000.

The hood scoop rams air into the engine's carburetor. Air mixes with fuel to add power to the car.

Safety features include an automatic fire extinguisher, special seatbelts, and an escape hatch in the roof.

Pro stock cars are designed to accelerate as fast as possible in a straight line. They must be based on regular street cars. The headlights, taillights, roof, and other features must resemble a factory model. Pro stock cars are not as fast as top fuel dragsters or funny cars, but they regularly top 200 miles (322 kilometers) per hour.

"Dyno Don" Nicholson built the first funny car in the mid-1960s. It had a strong drag racer frame. Nicholson covered the chassis with a lightweight body shell that looked like a production car. This shell could be flipped up for easy access to the car's insides. A reporter described this new design as "funny." The name "funny car" stuck.

FUNNY CARS

Funny cars are supposed to resemble the street cars they are designed after.

Safety features include an escape hatch in the roof.

Race teams add fin-like spoilers to the back of funny cars to help cars grip the track.

Supercharged engines and nitromethane fuel push funny cars to more than 300 miles (483 kilometers) per hour.

Funny cars also shoot out parachutes to help them slow down.

WHAT'S UNDER THE HOOD: TYPES OF ENGINES

hemi: *burns fuel in bowl-shaped chambers and produces more power than a regular engine*

supercharger: *forces more air and fuel into the cylinder to create more pressure and release more power*

turbocharger: *uses the engine's exhaust gases to spin a turbine; the system crams more air into the cylinder to boost an engine's power by 30 to 40 percent.*

rotary engine: *creates the power of an engine twice its size because the cylinder rotates around the crankshaft; in most engines, the crankshaft rotates around the cylinder.*

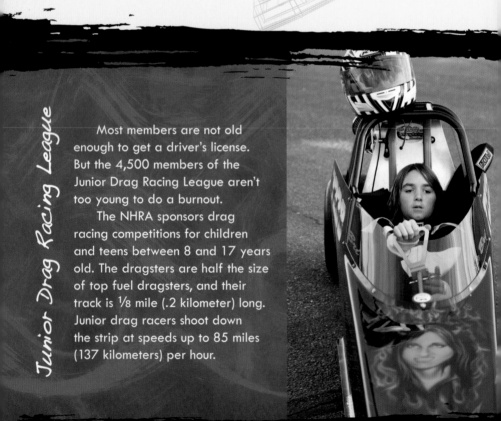

Junior Drag Racing League

Most members are not old enough to get a driver's license. But the 4,500 members of the Junior Drag Racing League aren't too young to do a burnout.

The NHRA sponsors drag racing competitions for children and teens between 8 and 17 years old. The dragsters are half the size of top fuel dragsters, and their track is ⅛ mile (.2 kilometer) long. Junior drag racers shoot down the strip at speeds up to 85 miles (137 kilometers) per hour.

Electric Dragsters

Not all dragsters roar and give off exhaust. Electric hot rods are quiet, pollution-free cars that run on batteries.

The National Electric Drag Racing Association (NEDRA) was formed in 1997 to organize electric hot rod races. They hold between three and five events each year.

Electric hot rods get faster each year. Roderick "Wildman" Wilde has pushed his electric "Maniac Mazda" up to 111 miles (179 kilometers) per hour.

Electric car racers call themselves "ampheads." They want to show the world that electric vehicles can save fuel and burn rubber at the same time.

DRAGSTER 1/4-MILE
SPEED RECORDS

Class	Driver	Speed	Year
Top fuel dragster	Tony Schumacher	336 mph (541 kmph)	2005
Funny car	Jack Beckman	334 mph (538 kmph)	2006
Pro stock car	Jason Line	212 mph (341 kmph)	2007

RACECARS FOR THE LONG HAUL

Emile Levassor

The 1895 Paris-Bordeaux-Paris Rally was one of the first rally races in motorsports. It was a 732-mile (1,178-kilometer) round-trip race on public roads. The drivers started in Paris and headed toward the French city of Bordeaux. There, a new driver was supposed to take over for the return trip to Paris.

Emile Levassor was the first racer to arrive in Bordeaux. He pulled into the city in the middle of the night, way ahead of schedule. But no one knew where his replacement driver was sleeping.

Levassor calmly got back in his racecar. He drove the entire way back to Paris. He easily came in first place with an average speed of 15 miles (24 kilometers) per hour. Levassor had driven 48 hours and 48 minutes all by himself!

RALLY RACES

Rallies are car races that take place on public or private roads. Drivers race from one point to another point. Usually two drivers take turns driving and navigating. If they have a mechanical problem, they often have to fix it themselves.

Most rallies are organized in stages. The cars leave at regular intervals. They race against the clock to the next destination. Professional rally races are usually judged on how quickly the cars get through the stages.

FAMOUS RALLIES:

Dakar Rally
Swedish Rally
Welsh Rally
Monte Carlo Rally (pictured)

RALLY CARS

Pro stage rallies are intense. Drivers race hundreds or thousands of miles over concrete, gravel, sand, snow, and ice.

Rally cars must be able to speed along open roads. But they must also have the suspension and handling to take on sharp curves.

Carmakers love to see their cars do well in road rallies. It shows car buyers that their vehicles are tough and reliable. In past years, successful rally cars have included the Mini Cooper, Audi Quattro, Ford Focus, and Subaru Impreza. Various models of Peugeots, Citroëns, and Porsches have also earned respect as rally cars.

The Arctic Trophy Rally is the world's longest rally race. It covers 9,942 miles (16,000 kilometers).

SMALLER SPEEDSTERS

Racing is not just for big, expensive cars. It also includes smaller racers. If it has wheels and an engine, it can race.

KARTS

Racecar designer Art Ingels was just fooling around. He welded together a few steel tubes. He added four wheels and put a lawn mower engine behind the seat. The go-kart was born. That was in 1956. Today, go-karts are simply called karts.

Karts have made a place for themselves on the track. There are more than 75,000 karters in the United States. Drivers can be as young as 5. As kids, pro drivers Jeff Gordon, Tony Stewart, and Danica Patrick raced karts.

Drivers must wear helmets, driving suits, and other safety gear.

Karts sit close to the ground. Most weigh about 150 pounds (68 kilograms). They are about 6 feet (1.8 meters) long and 4 feet (1.2 meters) wide. Engines range from 5 to 30 horsepower.

Before Jeff Gordon (right) became a famous NASCAR driver, he honed his skills racing karts and sprint cars (pictured).

There are two basic types of karts in racing. Sprint karts are the most popular type. They can reach speeds of 35 to 80 miles (56 to 129 kilometers) per hour. Enduro karts are higher-powered karts. They race on tracks for full-size cars. Enduro karts can reach more than 100 miles (161 kilometers) per hour.

RACING JOBS

Think you might like to work on a racing team someday? You could do more than just drive. Dozens of people work behind the scenes to get racecars ready for the big race.

Mechanic: *tunes the racecar for its best performance*

Painter: *uses paint and decals to make the cars look their best*

Electronics engineer: *works with a vehicle's computers and other complex electronics*

Aerodynamics engineer: *creates a sleek car that will slice through the air*

Energizer

CHARGER

Pit crew member: *fuels up car and makes minor adjustments and repairs during pit stops*

Public relations representative: *arranges media interviews with the driver and promotes the racing team*

DWARF AND LEGEND CARS

Dwarf and legend cars are built to look like classic stock cars from the 1930s and 1940s. But they are about half the size of the real cars.

The big difference between dwarf and legend cars is on the outside. Dwarf cars have no fenders to cover their wheels, and legend cars do.

legend car race

Like karts, dwarf and legend cars are cheaper ways to compete in racing. They can also be a step toward the big leagues. NASCAR stars Dale Earnhardt Jr. and Kyle Busch were both legend car racers.

Both dwarf and legend cars use mid-size motorcycle engines. These engines can power the car to speeds of 100 miles (161 kilometers) per hour.

SPRINT CARS

Sprint cars are stripped-down racers with big horsepower. These cars race on short dirt or paved tracks. Races are intense battles with plenty of bumping and banging.

Sprint cars slide into and out of corners at extreme angles. They use tires of different sizes to help them turn. This set-up is called "stagger."

Most sprint cars also have large wings. The wings give drivers more control.

Today's sprint cars require roll cages to protect the driver.

No matter their shape, size, or power, cars and racing go together. NASCAR champ Richard Petty said it best when he joked, "There is no doubt about precisely when folks began racing each other in automobiles. It was the day they built the second automobile."

45

GLOSSARY

airfoil (AYR-foyl) — a winglike feature attached to the back of a dragster to push the back end down

carburetor (KAR-buh-ray-tor) — the part of an engine where air and gasoline mix

chassis (CHASS-ee) — the frame on which the body of a vehicle is built

decal (DEE-kal) — a picture or label that can be transferred to hard surfaces

horsepower (HORSS-pou-ur) — a unit for measuring an engine's power

hot rod (HOT ROD) — a customized car or pickup

nitromethane (nye-troh-MEH-thane) — a mix of nitric acid and propane gas used as fuel in some dragsters

shell (SHELL) — the hard outer covering over the engine of a funny car

super speedway (SOO-pur SPEED-way) — a paved racetrack that is more than one and one-half mile long

traction (TRAK-shuhn) — the grip of a car's tires on the ground

wheelbase (WEEL-bayss) — the distance between a car's front and rear axles

READ MORE

Abramson, Andra Serlin. *Race Cars Up Close.* New York: Sterling, 2008.

Egan, Erin. *Hottest Race Cars.* Berkeley Heights, N.J.: Enslow, 2008.

Gifford, Clive. *The Kingfisher Racing: the Ultimate Motorsports Encyclopedia.* Boston: Kingfisher, 2006.

Koehler, Susan. *Race Car Crew Chief.* Jobs that Rock. Abbotsford, Victoria, Australia: Rourke, 2009.

INTERNET SITES

FactHound offers a safe, fun way to find Internet sites related to this book. All of the sites on FactHound have been researched by our staff.

Here's all you do:

Visit *www.facthound.com*

FactHound will fetch the best sites for you!

INDEX